Cursive Handwriting Workbook for Girls

Julie Harper

Cursive Handwriting Workbook for Girls

Cover Design by Melissa Stevens
www.theillustratedauthor.net
Write. Create. Illustrate.

Children's Books > Education & Reference > Words & Language

Children's Books > Education & Reference > Education > Workbooks

ISBN 10: 1490515712

EAN 13: 978-1490515717

Table of Contents

Introduction

The goal of this workbook is to inspire girls' interest in learning and practicing cursive handwriting. Girls enjoy reading girlish phrases like "pajama party" and inspirational or motivational sentences like, "Our generation is ready to change the world." Exercises like these help to make learning fun, whether in the classroom or at home.

This Cursive Handwriting Workbook for Girls focuses on writing phrases and sentences in cursive. Students who need more practice writing individual letters or single words may benefit from using this workbook in combination with a basic cursive writing workbook which focuses on practicing letters and short words.

Three sections of this workbook help students develop their cursive writing skills in three parts:

- ✓ Part 1 has mostly short phrases. Students trace and copy the words.
- ✓ The phrases become longer in Part 2. There are a couple of sentences and shorter phrases in Part 2, also, such that the transitions are not too abrupt. Students trace and copy the words.
- ✓ Part 3 advances onto sentences. At this stage, there is no tracing.

May your students or children improve their handwriting skills and enjoy reading and writing these girlish phrases and sentences.

Uppercase Cursive Alphabet

A B C D E F

G H I J K L

M N O P Q R

S T U V W X

Y Z

❤ ᵥ ❤

Lowercase Cursive Alphabet

a   b   c   d   e   f

g   h   i   j   k   l

m   n   o   p   q   r

s   t   u   v   w   x

y   z

Part 1 Short Phrases

Part 1 Instructions: First trace each word and then copy the words onto the blank line below.

Girlicious!

_____

Princess

_____

Glamour!

_____

Magical

_____

Skipping along!

Extraordinary

Heavenly!

Giggling

So sweet!

Fairy tale

Sparkly

Cheerful

Beautiful

It's shiny!

Good luck!

Wink, wink

Too cute!

Love it!

Pretty butterfly

Life is fun.

Go team!

Shine with confidence.

No problem!

Summer is sweet.

Beach party

Thoughtful

Fashionista

Gymnastics

Sportsmanship

Togetherness

Sisterhood

Friendship

Pajama party

Girl power!

Surprise me!

Big heart

Yes I can!

Nail art

Fun time

All my love!

_____
- -
_____

Skeptical

_____
- -
_____

You go girl!

_____
- -
_____

Team work

_____
- -
_____

I'm happy

_____
- -
_____

Self-worth

Dazzling

Quiet time

Happy thoughts

Love and laughter

Love and cherish

Water slides

Sunny days!

After school sports

Play hard

World peace

A better tomorrow

Promising future

Just add glitter

Love that color!

My playlist

Zest for life!

Freedom rings

Surfer girl

I can do anything

Tweens rule!

Don't worry

Beaded jewelry

Too, too funny!

Laugh it off!

Fun and games

Are you serious?

Tiara, bling, fashion

Slumber party tonight

Girl Scout cookies

Team spirit

Movie night

Trampoline bouncing

I know I can!

Over and out!

No big deal!

I'm tickled pink!

Endless possibilities

Lock and key

End of story!

Soccer girl

Family time

Just kidding!

In real life

Time will tell

Be yourself!

Proud of me!

Teach me how

Summer camp

As it should be!

Stand tall

I love myself!

Little dreamer

Non-judgmental

Have a good one!

Arts and crafts

Rock stars rock!

Forever friend!

For real?

How cool is that?

Feeling strong!

Always optimistic!

What's for dinner?

Real crocodile tears

Love you forever!

Natural beauty

Imagine peace.

Glitz and glam

Scent of a flower

Pep and cheer! Rah!

So happy I'm crying!

Laugh out loud!

Absolutely, positively

Love your smile

Stay strong

Give it your best

Tender-hearted

Chocolate lover!

Sleep all day

Dance all night!

Friday night sleepover

Quiet, please.

Noses love perfume

My bad! Oops!

Imagine that

Take your time.

Faith and hope

Baton twirling

Show you care

Positive attitude!

Enjoy today

Be content

Sporty and lively

Tennis ace!

Private time, please!

I love myself

Hot fudge sundae

Respect yourself

No bad hair days!

Take it slowly

Hugs and kisses

Thinking of you!

School is so cool.

We can do it.

Chuckle and grin

Part 2 Longer Phrases

Part 2 Instructions: First trace each phrase and then copy the phrase onto the blank line below.

Sweet, sweet memories

Give me a hug.

Make new friends.

Double cheeseburger for me

It's my cuddly teddy bear.

Make the best of it.

Shine bright

Rock 'n roll, baby

My fingers are crossed.

Can't wait to see you!

Mom's baby girl forever!

Try to understand

Ballerina dancing

Just having fun!

Charming personality

Exclusive: for girls only!

Pizza for breakfast!

Love who you are.

Happiness glows.

Maybe. Maybe not.

Out of this world

Best friends forever!

Please explain that.

Hit it out of the park!

Inner beauty rules!

Bubbly and bouncy

Give a compliment.

Don't even go there!

Country fair days are fun.

Giggling out loud

You can't be serious!

Yes, I'm proud of myself.

Just wondering?

Grin and bear it.

Sh... I hugged my teddy.

See you around. Later!

Maybe one of these days.

Laugh to myself!

Fill in the blanks.

Girls will be girls!

Soar like an eagle.

For your eyes only...

We're in it together.

Give it your best shot.

Wild hair day

Mismatched socks are cool.

Shop until you drop.

Flavored lip gloss. . .

Laugh until you cry!

Just joking around...

Tell me it isn't so!

Give me a hint, please.

Don't make me cry!

If you only knew...

Reach for the moon.

Stretch your wings.

You have to be kidding!

Hang out at the mall.

Same place, same time.

Just give me candy.

Put on a happy face!

Chocolate chip cookies. Yum!

Bursting with laughter!

Weekend night owl.

Challenge your mind!

Love the little things.

Share a friendship bracelet.

Enjoy a good book.

I made it all by myself!

Hanging with friends

Are we having fun yet?

Digital guardian angel

Twinkling starlight

Follow your dreams!

My own personality

Keep a secret forever.

Just be yourself!

Thank you very much!

I did it all by myself!

Love you like a sister

Private. Keep out.

No reply necessary

Future, here I come!

Talking to myself

Please press rewind.

Be true to yourself!

Daddy's little girl forever!

Walking in the rain

Frilly pink girl stuff

Love flip flops and sweats

It's fun to accessorize.

Don't worry about it!

My sister, my friend

Balloons and confetti

Run your heart out

I love surprise parties!

Be your own true self.

Just hanging with friends.

You are fabulous!

Looking forward to it

Determined and focused

Sequins, glitter, and frills

My home is my castle.

Kindness is contagious.

My dad, the ATM machine

Shiny, shimmering hearts

Super dazzling personality

Too much information!

Keep it short and simple.

Believe in miracles.

Smiling and fun-loving

Carefree and confident

Truth, trust, and loyalty

I'm so proud of you!

Catch a shooting star.

I'll give it my best shot.

You're on a roll today.

If you know what I mean

Always love seeing friends

Awkward moments are fine.

Just having a good day!

Pom poms and cheers

My doggie loves her shiny

rhinestone collar!

What was I thinking?

Just me and my teddy

Explore your creative side.

Where's my saxophone?

Double Dutch jump rope

Where's my magic wand?

Some guidance, please.

Tomorrow is another day!

Can green M & M's be

considered a vegetable?

Cheer until you're hoarse.

Watching my favorite show

Double decker school bus

Great big hugs and kisses

Enter at your own risk.

Flowers in my hair

A twinkle in my eye

Always in my heart

Girls dream in color.

Grinning from ear to ear

My mom, my superhero

Think happy thoughts.

Listen with compassion.

All-star girls rule.

I found the key to success.

Hey, no Paparazzi allowed.

Pop, jazz, and funky music

My schedule is full.

Forever in my heart

Riding my horse to school

Friday night pajama party

Pillow fights are sweet.

Roll on the floor laughing.

I love spending time

with my friends.

Let me read, please.

It's a mystery.

My sweet personal diary

Private: Do not enter.

Show respect at all times.

Yummy after school snack

Homemade cookies

Fresh out of the oven

Delicious and scrumptious

Yummy for my tummy!

Sticky sweet cotton candy

Pink sandwiches with pink

lemonade, and cupcakes

Breakfast in bed on my

birthday. So very nice!

Running in circles

Screaming, hollering at

the top of my lungs!

Just kidding! Ha ha!

Please, thank you, welcome

Calling all girls.

Dream and be inspired.

The power of confidence

It's okay to be yourself.

Always be true to yourself.

Beauty comes from within.

We are all beautiful!

Be proud of who you are.

You are special.

Be the best you can be.

Part 3 Sentences

Part 3 Instructions: Copy these sentences onto the blank lines. (There is no tracing in Part 3.)

It's three-o'clock in the

morning. Why do I

suddenly remember the

answer to the test question?

Who said I can't do it?

I just proved you wrong!

Endless possibilities are

in store for me!

Yes, I can do it!

Save the earth – recycle.

Plant a vegetable garden.

Don't be a litterbug!

Reuse, and don't waste.

Walk, or ride your bicycle.

On a snowy day in

January, build a snowman

with a happy face.

Drink hot chocolate in

front of the fireplace.

Snuggle up and watch your

favorite movie while eating

hot buttered popcorn.

What should I do next?

Texting, instead of talking.

Our generation is ready

to change the world!

It's smooth sailing from

here on out.

Pick me up if I stumble.

Which way is up?

Be like Alice in Wonderland

once in a while, and

imagine something fantastic.

Goofiness is so silly!

Is my bed a trampoline?

Jumping jacks at eight in

the morning on Saturday.

Stay in touch with us.

I love to make you smile!

I like reading under the

covers with a flashlight.

We watched our favorite

movie for the tenth time!

Read my t-shirt!

Silly boys! Skateboards

are for girls.

Just cruising through my

neighborhood on my bike.

Having fun, fun, fun!

Imagine if magic were real.

What cool things would

you learn in school?

What classes would you

take? Fun to imagine...

It's almost my birthday!

Hopscotch with my friends...

Sunday afternoon is our

family time!

Running through the rain...

Zillions of twinkling stars

in the night sky are

winking at me!

Where is Santa Claus?

I want cookies and milk.

Smile, grin, and smirk.

No frowns or pouts.

Laugh, chuckle, and giggle.

Glow, beam, and radiate.

Spread happiness.

Hair. Oh my hair. How

should I wear my hair?

Short, long, straight, or

curly? Braids, a twist,

a bun, or ponytails?

In such a happy mood!

Happy, bouncy, animated,

cheery, and delightful.

Woke up on the wrong side

of the bed. Grumpy!

Happiness is mom and

me having a girls day out.

Lunch for two...

Matinee movie and candy.

Shopping, talking, laughing.

Yum! Making my

favorite cookies from scratch.

Quiet time listening to

my top hundred songs. . .

Simply heavenly!

Is there really a pot of

gold at the end of the

rainbow? Let's find out!

Singing and dancing in the

rain on the way to school.

I love my friends...

Spending time at the mall...

Meet me at the food court.

It's a happy day for us!

Relax and enjoy!

You make the world

beautiful. Yes, you do!

A nature walk on a

cloudy summer morning.

Swim like a mermaid.

Little girls grow up to

become beautiful women.

I found the keys to success.

Top girl, top performer!

Enjoy your day!

Pomeranian puppies are

so very adorable!

Horseback riding on a

sunny summer afternoon.

Giddy up, horsey!

Life is beautiful!

You are beautiful!

I am beautiful!

Cool girls are true to

themselves and friends.

A frown is an upside

down smile. Smile!

Ah-choo! Gesundheit!

Sticking it out!

Dream catcher.

Everyone is good at

something. Remember that.

Always believe in yourself.

Give yourself a break.

How am I doing so far?

It's a dream vacation.

Another day in paradise...

Relax and enjoy it

while it lasts.

Spend time with family.

Falling off my chair

laughing so hard...

I've got nothing but love

for my family and friends.

How can I help you?

She has a twinkle in her

eye when she's happy!

Hey! What you see is

what you get!

Rah! Rah! Rah! Let's go!

Whispering silly stories...

Goofy times are fun!

Take a picture... It will

last longer! Say cheese!

Don't cry! Be happy!

You are strong.

Dream big.

Dreams can become reality.

Do you want to celebrate?

Let's dance!

Beauty salon appointment...

Shampoo and conditioner...

Comb, brush, and mirror...

Hair dryer, curling iron...

Styling gel or hair spray?

School is out for summer

break. All set for vacation.

My bags are packed.

Riding the waves on a

warm sunny day in June...

Such a cute dimple when

she smiles.

Turn a frown into a smile.

We are so amazing.

Go girls! We can do it!

Team players and good

sportsmanship are an

unbeatable combination.

Practice and play hard!

Learn from your losses!

A rainbow, cloudy skies...

Splish splashing through

the puddles on a rainy day

in May wearing a flowered

slicker and rain boots...

Camping out in my

backyard telling ghost stories.

Chocolate, graham crackers

plus marshmallows equals

S'mores. Yummy!

Fun things to do in August:

Decorate your sidewalk

with colorful chalk...

Learn to windsurf...

Have a treasure hunt...

County fair days...

Prizes – Teddy bears...

Fun rides, gooey food...

Best in show blue ribbon...

Pinball and arcade games...

Cheerleader and team

captain of basketball, golf,

volleyball, soccer, hockey,

baseball, water polo, and

tennis...

Shall we walk, run, skip,

or hop? Play hop scotch,

four-square or dodge ball?

Ride the merry-go-round

or swing at the park?

You are invited to my

birthday party.

Come dressed in a costume.

Prizes will be given to

the best costumes.

Let's go on a scavenger

hunt. The team who

finds the most items

will be awarded a prize.

Happy hunting!

Mars needs girls.

It's around one hundred

forty million miles from

Earth to Mars! Wow!

You go, girl!

Wake up ready to have a

great day. Do your best to

make it happen. Don't let

any problems bring you

down. Stay positive.

My bedroom is my

personal space to play,

daydream, and sleep.

It's my very own design

and style!

Life is an amazing

journey. Enjoy it!

You can make a difference.

Find your motivation.

Work toward your goals.

This summer, we are

going to show movies

in our backyard. Our

neighbors are all invited.

Don't forget the popcorn.

I get to play miniature

golf using my favorite

colored golf ball. I hope I

get a hole-in-one!

The castle is so cool!

Once upon a time...

Fairy tales can come true.

Wish upon a star.

And they lived happily

ever after.

I get around town on

my little pink scooter.

It's smooth gliding and

sure to get me to my best

friend's house.

It's fun to take nature

walks and explore the

great outdoors. There

are so many things to

see and learn.

My friends and I like

to see who can jump rope

the longest without

stepping on the rope.

One, two, three, four...

I'm afraid my teacher

won't believe that my

poodle really ate my

homework! What

should I do?

Cursive writing is fun!

Congratulations!

You made it!

Sign your name below.

Your name is _____.

Other Workbooks by Julie Harper

✓ Letters, Words, and Silly Phrases Handwriting Workbook (Reproducible): Practice Writing in Cursive (Second and Third Grade).

✓ Wacky Sentences Handwriting Workbook (Reproducible): Practice Writing in Cursive (Third and Fourth Grade).

✓ Print Uppercase and Lowercase Letters, Words, and Silly Phrases: Kindergarten and First Grade Writing Practice Workbook (Reproducible).

✓ Print Wacky Sentences: First and Second Grade Writing Practice Workbook (Reproducible).

81619505R00072

Made in the USA
Lexington, KY
18 February 2018